THE AUSTIN MUSIC SCENE

1965–1994

THROUGH THE LENS OF BURTON WILSON

Burton Wilson
with Jack Ortman

EAKIN PRESS Austin, Texas

For CIP information,
please access:
www.loc.gov

Design/typography by
Amber Stanfield

Edited by
Angela Buckley

FIRST EDITION
Copyright © 2001 by Burton Wilson
Published in the United States of America
By Eakin Press
A division of Sunbelt Media, Inc.
P.O. Drawer 90159
Austin, Texas 78709-0159
email: eakinpub@sig.net
website: www.eakinpress.com
ALL RIGHTS RESERVED.
1   2   3   4   5   6   7   8   9
1-57168-444-1

THANKS TO

Clifford Antone
Marcia Ball
Miriam Blum
Doug Brown
Mike Buck
Chet Flippo
Jim Franklin
Doug Hanners
Freddie Krc
Emma Little
Carlyne Majer

George Majewski
Larry Monroe
Margaret Moser
Tracy Nelson
Derek O'Brien
Donna Pearl
Spencer Perskin
Charlie Pritchard
Micael Priest
Al Ragle
Paul Ray

Gilbert Shelton
Bobby Earl Smith
Angela Strehli
Jay Trachtenberg
John Wheat
Houston White
Eddie Wilson
Minor Wilson

And to all the musicians and fans
who have made Austin
the "Live Music Capital of the World."

FOREWORD

August 1970: "Hello, my name is Burton Wilson, and I am a free lance photographer. I take a lot of photographs of musicians, and if you will be so kind as to allow me access to Armadillo World Headquarters, I will make available to you copies of any pictures I shoot."

Sounded like a good deal to me. Sounded clear and solid, an articulate and mature sound. First sound like that I'd heard in weeks. I was twenty-six years old and I'd been in the rock-and-roll business since June. Most of the people I came in contact with were younger than I was. Chaos, noise, and unnecessary urgency surrounded me. This guy was calm, quiet, very collected. Burton was coming on fifty. Twice our age.

I said, "Burton, you've got a great name. Just tell anybody that asks that you own the place. That way, you'll never need a backstage pass."

December 1999: I just turned fifty-six, and seeing Burton almost every day is what keeps me from getting the blues about it. Burton has always made it cool to be older. During the hippie heyday at the Armadillo, he also made it cool to be polite and precise, and he taught some of us perspective by example. He recorded the rest of us as we scurried about, overwrought, overworked, and worried that we would go to hell if we turned a nickel too much profit. We were wrong, of course, about everything but the burning desire to do right. Burton truly loved us just as we were, and that knowledge gradually made us very proud: "This is the coolest old dude that we've ever met, and he thinks *we're* something special!" He was more special than we thought.

Burton came and went freely in his neat and tidy way. Slowly, we realized that he was having far more fun than all the rest of us combined. He didn't just chronicle what we did; he did it with us. He just went home at a decent hour. We aged. He didn't.

Over the years, Burton has continued to act like he owns the place. For twenty years, it's been a different place, Threadgill's Restaurant instead of the Armadillo. They are similar because he's here. He's in the restaurant every morning before we open. He makes his own coffee if he's too early. We share our notes when they are funny. He hears my wildest schemes before they are launched. Many have not been launched, because my telling of them seemed to stir Burton too little, so that I had to reevaluate the merit of the schemes. He never holds back his enthusiasm if I manage to capture it, and his encouragement, his criticism, and his advice are among my most valued assets.

Sometimes when I look at the photos Burton has made of the events in my life, I wax silly about him becoming my life preserver. These pictures are worth far more to me than a mere thousand words apiece. I can't hope to render them in print, but I love the soundtrack they provide me when I gaze at them awhile, lock in my memory, and hear again the conversations that were taking place. Because of Burton's photos, I can still hear Jerry Garcia listening to Doug Sahm talk a mile a minute. I can hear Roy Buchanan and Bill Monroe and Mance Lipscomb and Freddie King, and

many more I'd never hear again if it weren't for Burton. The voices of forgetten cohorts and the music of long-gone legends are mine because of him.

Thank you, Burton, for all these memories and many more that'll never make it into a book.

*At Armadillo World Headquarters
April 13, 1972*

—Eddie Wilson
Armadillo World Headquarters (1970–1980)
Threadgill's Restaurant (1981–)

I have been interested in hot jazz and blues ever since I was a student at the Rhode Island School of Design in the late 1930s. Playing jazz and blues records was very popular among a few students, and I took right to it. I read Hughes Panassic's *Le Jazz Hot*, which was published in France in 1934, and I agreed with him that jazz and blues music were important contributions to American culture.

Through the years, wherever I happened to be, I would search for used 78 rpm records in secondhand stores. They would come in with old phonograph cabinets, and the shop owners were always happy to sell them for five cents each. In a big stack of used records, I could almost always find a few that were worth buying. Some were badly worn, but most of them were in good condition. The great thing about this was that it gave me countless recordings of unrecognized—and sometimes completely forgotten—blues artists like Leroy Carr, Peetie Wheatstraw, Doctor Clayton, Elijah Jones, Big Bill Johnson (a pseudonym for Big Bill Broonzy), Blind Teddy Darby, Georgia White, Alfoncy Harris, and dozens of others.

The Barker Texas History Center (now the Center for American History) at the University of Texas in Austin heard about my collection and asked if they could tape part of it for their archives. I agreed—if they would give me copies of the tapes. I don't know what percentage of my collection they taped, but they made 38 seven-inch reels that have 836 records on them.

At their request, I gave my collection of 78 rpm records to the University of Texas for their archives. It was a stack of records ten feet tall.

A lot of jazz and blues has been reissued on LP records. I have 85 ten-inch albums. Ten-inch LP records haven't been produced since the early 1960s. I have well over a hundred twelve-inch albums.

In the mid-1960s, the University of Texas built a new Fine Arts building and offered a course of study in photography. I got my academic credits and enrolled as an undergraduate student. I took four semesters under the supervision of Russell Lee, a world-famous photographer.

When I got out, some young people had started a concert hall in downtown Austin called the Vulcan Gas Company. It featured a "light show" and rock-and-roll bands from around the country. Between these concerts, they had programs of old southern blues performers. I was interested in all of the music they presented, but more in the blues than any other kind.

After a few years, that club closed; but, at the same time, Armadillo World Headquarters opened in South Austin on Barton Springs Road. They featured a variety of entertainment, from rock-and-roll bands to stage plays, and they also included blues concerts.

I came and went at the Armadillo as I pleased and became the house photographer. I spent a lot of time taking pictures of the musicians. It was a thrill to meet some of those older musicians whose records I had listened to when I was in school.

It was a pleasure to work at these clubs, because the music was always good and all of the personnel treated me with such respect.

Work doesn't get any better than that.

FEATURED VENUES

ANTONE'S
Sixth and Brazos
(currently at 213 West Fifth Street)
Austin, Texas

ARMADILLO WORLD HEADQUARTERS
525 Barton Springs Road
Austin, Texas

ASCOT ROOM
East Eleventh Street
Austin, Texas

BEVO'S
2313 Rio Grande Street
Austin, Texas

CASTLE CREEK
1411 Lavaca Street
Austin, Texas

CHEQUERED FLAG
1411 Lavaca Street
Austin, Texas

CITY COLISEUM
101 Dawson Street
Austin, Texas

FILLMORE AUDITORIUM
Fillmore and Geary
San Francisco, California

THE HUNGRY HORSE
Trinity and Eighteenth streets
Austin, Texas

LA ZONA ROSA
612 West Fourth Street
Austin, Texas

MATRIX
3138 Fillmore
San Francisco, California

MENLO JUNIOR COLLEGE
Menlo Park, California

NEW ORLEANS CLUB
1125 Red River Street
Austin, Texas

PALMER AUDITORIUM
400 South First Street
Austin, Texas

PEASE PARK
1100 Kingsbury Street
Austin, Texas

ROLLING HILLS
Bee Caves Road at Walsh Tarlton Lane
Austin, Texas

SOAP CREEK SALOON No. 1
Bee Caves Road at Walsh Tarlton Lane
Austin, Texas

THREADGILL'S
6416 North Lamar Boulevard
Austin, Texas

VICTORY GRILL
1104 East Eleventh Street
Austin, Texas

VULCAN GAS COMPANY
316 Congress Avenue
Austin, Texas

WOOLDRIDGE PARK
812 Guadalupe
Austin, Texas

Mance Lipscomb

At Tary Owens' Home
Austin, Texas
November 13, 1965

I first met Mance Lipscomb on November 13, 1965, at Tary Owens' apartment on Grandview Street in Austin. Tary has always been interested in the revival of all authentic blues and would drive a hundred miles to Navasota to pick Mance up. Mance would stay at Tary's house for the weekend when performing at some local club. Tary invited me to meet Mance one afternoon and listen to him play his guitar and sing the blues.

Mance Lipscomb

At Home in Navasota, Texas
February 15, 1967

Tary Owens called me and said he was going to drive to Mance's house in Navasota with a writer named Jim Langdon, who wanted to write an article about Mance. He asked me if I would like to go along. I said, "You bet," and grabbed my camera.

When we arrived, Mance introduced us to his wife, Elnora, and his grand-daughter, Annie. We wandered around his place on the edge of town and then drove around the countryside. He loved to talk and told us about everything as we drove by—fields where he had worked, the school his kids went to, the dance halls where he had performed, and houses where he had played for "rent parties," where people would dance and have a good time and chip in to pay the rent.

When we got to town, he asked Tary to drive to a store that had a post office in it, where he got his mail. When he got out of the car, he said it was a good store, and did any of us want to buy anything? We said no, we didn't, but he sort of lingered, so I jumped out saying that I did need something. He led me into the store and with pride introduced me to everyone who was in it, saying, "This is Burton Wilson, a photographer from Austin who has come to do a story about me." I enjoyed that so much and have always been proud that I gave him that moment of glory.

We went back to the house and had lunch. The four of us sat at the small kitchen table, and Elnora served the food. It was very good. She put two meat dishes on the table; one was fried chicken, and I helped myself to that. Along with it were boiled potatoes and turnip greens—you just can't miss with those.

From the kitchen table, we moved to the living room, and Mance picked up his guitar. He played and sang song after song. I don't know how to describe it, but heaven hasn't got a chance of being any better.

Between songs he would rest his guitar and talk. He would look far away and in a gentle voice would say, "I wrote this next song when—", and he would go into detail about where he was and what prompted him to write it. He said he could play and sing more than three hundred songs and had written most of them himself. In all sincerity I said, "Mance, how do you write a song?" Without hesitating, he looked at me and said, "First, you've got to start." I have never forgotten that moment and have lived with that piece of advice ever since, and use it often.

The light was very good, and I took a lot of photographs. They have been used many times since for album and video covers, books, magazines, and posters. Jim Franklin, the great Texas poster artist, liked them and used them several times, because they were the only pictures of Mance taken when he wasn't wearing a hat. Mance always wore a felt hat wherever he was, and that included on a concert stage.

At one time, he was flying all over the country to perform in jazz and blues concerts like Newport, Berkeley, and others. I asked him if he liked to fly, and he said, "No, I don't like it at all, but there isn't any other way to get there. I just sit by the aisle and look at the floor and pretend I'm on a train. The only trouble is that the captain gets on the P.A. system and says we are flying 32,000 feet high. I wish he wouldn't do that, because nobody cares how high they are flying, and it scares me."

Conqueroo

At a love-in
Wooldridge Park
Austin, Texas
April 15, 1967

Originally St. John and the Conqueroo, they were founded in the mid-sixties by Powell St. John, who left shortly thereafter for San Francisco. Ed Guinn and Bob Brown continued the band and played regularly at the Vulcan and at events such as the love-in at Wooldridge Park (reputed to be the first such event in the Southwest).

The Conqueroo was one of Austin's first psyche-delic rock bands. Although their total recorded output amounted to only one 45 single, their strength was in live performances.

Ed Guinn, Charlie Pritchard,
Wali "Oat Willie" Stopher, Bob Brown

Bob Brown and Charlie Pritchard

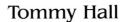

Tommy Hall

Love-in at Pease Park
April 16, 1967

During the mid-sixties, the 13th Floor Elevators, a small rock band with blatant overtones of drug consciousness filling their music, gained an avid following in Austin. They are considered the very first psychedelic band, ahead of the Grateful Dead and the Jefferson Airplane. The group toured California in 1966, playing the Avalon and other clubs, and they were very popular with audiences.

The band consisted of Roky Erickson, guitar and vocal; Tommy Hall, electric jug; Benny Thurman, bass; Stacy Sutherland, lead guitar; and John Ike Walton, drums. The electric jug had a sound like no other instrument and was one of the more unusual aspects of the band.

Psychedelic rock was a completely new sound in music—I can't describe it other than to say it was forceful and loud and got your attention. You either liked it or hated it—there was no middle ground.

Around 1964 or 1965, my son Minor, Russell Wheelock, and Jamie Spence were building a thirty-two-foot trimaran in our backyard. A lot of people dropped by to see it and visit. One of them was Tommy Hall, the 13th Floor Elevators' founder.

I got to know Tommy very well, and one summer day he said they were playing that night at a hall on Houston Street and that he would leave my name at the door, so I went.

It was a small hall with a four-foot-high stage on one end that had stairs leading up to it. Behind the stage there was a small room. There was no air-conditioning, nor fans, and two sidewalls had four-by-eight-foot horizontal openings with panels locked in an open position.

When I got there, the band was going full blast and the hall was packed full of hippies, and they were all swaying to the beat of the music in what appeared to be some kind of hypnotic condition.

After a while, the band took a break and they all went to the little back room, except Tommy, who sat on the stairs with me. The entire crowd drifted outside to get a breath of fresh air, or maybe smoke something. Tommy and I chatted, and we were the only people remaining in the hall.

In ten or fifteen minutes, the band came back on the stage and picked up their instruments, and Tommy joined them. Roky mumbled something, stamped his foot twice, and they broke into one of their songs. It hit the audience lounging outside like a bolt of lightning, and in a fit of hysteria, they clamored to get back in. Many came through the door four at a time, while the others climbed through the open windows on top of each other like rats abandoning a burning ship. To this day, I can close my eyes, hear the Elevators, and see those people as they desperately fought their way back into that hall.

John Clay is a longtime Austin tradition who never really sought or gained wide recognition. Clay is interwoven with much of the Austin music scene. He played with his Lost Austin Band.

Tommy Hall and John Clay

Underground City Hall

1606 Lavaca Street, Austin, Texas
July 14, 1967

Gilbert Shelton (pictured above) writes: "Underground City Hall, Austin's notorious head shop, was opened by Joe E. Brown, Tony Bell, and myself around the beginning of 1968, using the money we got from *Wonder Wart-Hog Quarterly No. 1*. Our landlord was Dan's Liquor Store down at the corner. One day they told us we would have to paint over the day-glo chartreuse and black striped paint job on the front of our store, as one of their other tenants on the block was complaining that it was ruining the character of the street.

"We did not do a big business at first. The worst day for gross receipts was, as I remember, only $2.69, but that was enough for a bottle of vodka, Joe's minimum wage. Joe complained that he was spending all his time at the store, and therefore doing the bulk of the work, which led Tony and me to donate our interest in the enterprise to him. He sold it to Doug and Judy Brown and George Majewski shortly thereafter.

"Although the original name of the store was 'Underground City Hall,' when Wali Stopher proclaimed his campaign for the governorship of Texas, we gave him the second entrance to the shop (it had two doors onto the street) and nine square feet of floor space for him and his desk and, briefly, we called it 'Underground City Hall and Oat Willie's Campaign Headquarters.'

"The character 'Oat Willie' came from a phrase I saw written in Joe E. Brown's notebook, for which I drew the original character. Wali, much to everyone's delight, assumed this name for his astonishing political career (although he did run under his own name, as I recall, when he ran for mayor of Austin and finished a respectable fourth out of twenty some-odd candidates)."

Mother Earth

Fillmore Auditorium
San Francisco, California
September 1967

After leaving the Conqueroo in Austin, Powell St. John headed to San Francisco, where he teamed up with Tracy Nelson to form the nucleus of Mother Earth. For several years, Mother Earth was an important part of the Fillmore scene, combining rock with blues and a touch of country. After a while, St. John left the band, and Tracy Nelson became its prime force.

Powell St. John and Tracy Nelson

Sleepy John Estes

Vulcan Gas Company
April 19, 1968

I photographed Sleepy John Estes at the Vulcan on April 19, 1968. It was a real pleasure to meet and photograph him, because I remembered so well playing his 78s when I was at the Rhode Island School of Design.

He had been performing all of his life and played gigs anywhere he could throughout the South. His reputation grew somewhat through a few records, and he is now looked upon as one of the authentic southern bluesmen.

Otis Spann

Vulcan Gas Company
August 2, 1968
With Muddy Waters; Luther Johnson, guitar; and S. P. Leary, drums

Known primarily for his work with Muddy Waters, as when this photo was taken, Spann also played with most of the other legendary Chicago bluesmen. He also performed and recorded on his own, singing the vocals as well as playing piano.

Muddy Waters

Vulcan Gas Company
August 2, 1968

The first time I ever photographed at the Vulcan Gas Company was August 1968. The main attraction was the great Muddy Waters and his band, including Otis Spann on keyboards. They had been top performers singing the blues since the 1940s and had many R&B hits.

To explain just how tough it was to make a living making music at that time: Muddy and Otis and the whole band drove to Austin, all the way from Chicago, in two old station wagons, with equipment and all, just to play at the Vulcan for a two-night engagement. They did not have any other gigs along the way.

14 中

Johnny Winter Trio

Vulcan Gas Company
August 2, 1968
Johnny Winter, Uncle John Turner, Tommy Shannon

The Johnny Winter Trio from Beaumont was the opening act. That night became a part of music history when the unknown, skinny albino kid and his band stole the show. With his magic guitar and powerful, bluesy singing voice, Johnny drove that capacity audience right up the wall. As the evening wore on, they ignored Muddy Waters, who admittedly wasn't at his best, and chanted for more of the newfound musical genius from East Texas.

Muddy was the first to recognize what was happening and sharpened up his second set, but by then the night belonged to the Johnny Winter Trio.

Muddy and Johnny immediately became good friends and remained so. They recorded several albums together and were nominated for and won Grammy Awards for their collaborations.

Rock journalist Larry Sepulvado was in the audience, wrote a review of the show, and sent it to *Rolling Stone* magazine, who printed it in their next issue. The powers that be at Columbia Records read the story and grabbed him. It turned into one of those show-biz stories you heard about—"discovered in an obscure little dance hall and playing Broadway next week."

Call it an overnight discovery if you want to, but Johnny had been playing the guitar and singing professionally since the age of twelve. Anyplace he could find to play was good enough for him. He was born in Beaumont and started playing there and in Houston. Not being appreciated at all, he went to Chicago for a few years. In the early 1960s, when the

music scene got hot in London, he went there. London had "discovered" Jimi Hendrix and made him a top name, but that didn't happen for Johnny, so he returned to Houston.

Back in Houston Johnny formed his trio, with Tommy Shannon on bass and Uncle John Turner on drums.

There's an interesting roundabout story of how the Vulcan Gas Company learned about Johnny. The Conqueroo, who played as the house band at 316 Congress, played at the Family Dog in Denver and shared the bill there with the Johnny Winter Trio. When they came back to Austin, they raved about this sensational band. Houston White phoned Johnny and made arrangements for the trio to perform at the Vulcan.

Johnny, Uncle John, and Tommy rolled into Austin in an old hearse that sort of died in Houston's driveway. As they were an immediate hit, they stayed on and played many times at the Vulcan Gas Company.

Big Joe Williams

At The Victory Grill in East Austin
August 14, 1968

One morning, Houston White, the top guy at the Vulcan Gas Company, phoned me. He said Big Joe Williams, an old-time bluesman from Mississippi, was in town and would be performing at the Vulcan for the next two nights. He said he was going to take him to lunch and wanted to know if I would like to go along. This was in August 1968. I was fresh out of the University and hot on my new career, so I jumped at the chance.

We went to the rooming house where he was staying and met him. He was as friendly as could be and we got along wonderfully. The three of us chatted for a while and then went to lunch at a convenient café on East Eleventh Street.

We returned to the rooming house and spent all afternoon with Big Joe on the front porch. I kept my camera busy while he talked about his life, sang the blues, and played his nine-string guitar. To get an individual sound, he had taken a standard six-string guitar and added three strings to it.

It was an afternoon I would never forget. I shot picture after picture of poses I liked, and when I had only a few frames left, I asked him how he would like to pose for me. Without saying a word, he went to an abandoned auto in the vacant lot beside the house, opened the door, sat down, and played his guitar.

That told the whole story—how he had spent most of his life driving around the country from one gig to another playing his guitar in any bar, barrelhouse, or honky-tonk that would pay him to sing the blues.

The Lavender Hill Express

Vulcan Gas Company
October 3, 1968

Lavender Hill Express was an early creation of Rusty Wier's. Personnel included Jess Yaryan, bass; Leonard Arnold, guitar; John Schwertner, keyboards; Rusty Wier, drums; and Layton DePenning, guitar. With this group, Wier taped one album at the Vulcan Gas Company. After a year or so, Wier left the band and set out on his own as a folk-blues performer, becoming very popular in Austin. Wier achieved national acclaim with his album *Stoned, Slow, Rugged.*

Pure Funk Rock Band

Menlo Junior College, Menlo, California
October 1968
Tary Owens, bass; Peter Auschlin, drums;
Jamie Howell, guitar; Stan Portyes, guitar

The Fugs
Vulcan Gas Company
February 21, 1969
Ken Weaver, Peter Stampfel, Ed Sanders, Pete Kearney, Vinny Leary, Tuli Kupferberg

Jimmy Reed

Backstage at Vulcan Gas Company
March 14, 1969

A popular performer and recording artist, Reed's impact on blues and rock has been immense. Early in his career, he was caught between rock and pure blues forms, but as the two became more entwined during the sixties, his popularity and influence rose significantly. After a period of ill health, Reed had been performing again when he died suddenly in 1976.

Jim Mings and
Jimmy Reed

Don Lupo, bass; Jay Mead, drums; Jim Mings, guitar; Jimmy Reed, guitar/vocals and harmonica

New Atlantis

With Jomo Disaster Light Show at Vulcan Gas Company
March 21, 1969
Danny Galindo, bass; Jay Mead, drums; Jim Mings, guitar; Mike Read, piano

Big Mama Thornton

Vulcan Gas Company
March 21, 1969

Willie Mae Thornton was born and raised in Alabama. Her father was a minister and her mother sang in the church. She never took lessons, and she taught herself to sing and play the harmonica and drums. Willie Mae left home when she was fourteen and toured with the Hot Harlem Review out of Atlanta, and she remained with the show until 1948, when she went to Houston. During her stay in Houston, Big Mama met and observed many of the great bluesmen—Junior Parker, Lightnin' Hopkins, Lowell Fulson, Clarence "Gatemouth" Brown, and many others.

She was acclaimed for her recording of "Hound Dog," later made famous by Elvis Presley.

> *Jay Mead, drums; Bee Houston, guitar;*
> *Big Mama Thornton, vocals.*

Angela Strehli

Sunnyland Special
Wooldridge Park Love-in
April 13, 1969

Austin blues singer Angela Strehli teamed with harmonica player
Lewis Cowdrey in 1968 to form the rhythm-and-blues group The
Fabulous Rockets. By 1969 the group was known as Sunnyland
Special. In the early seventies, Angela toured Texas with James
Polk and the Brothers. Angela then formed another rhythm-and-
blues group, Hard Times, which eventually became Southern
Feeling. She now lives in California and is still performing.

Lewis Cowdrey, harmonica; Robert Franklin, guitar;
Angela Strehli, vocals; Richard Funnell, drums;
Jesse Taylor, bass

Angela Strehli and Houston White

Shiva's Headband

Love-in at Wooldridge Park, Austin, Texas
April 13, 1969
Spencer Perskin, Jerry Barnett,
Kenny Parker, Shawn Siegel

During the psychedelic era, Shiva's Headband reigned supreme in Austin and gained some attention during a short stay in San Francisco. The most prominent feature of the band was the driving, frenetic electric fiddle of Spencer Perskin. While Shiva's was most definitely electric and cosmic, the country influence was heavy in their music, making it extremely original.

Steve Miller

Vulcan Gas Company
May 12, 1969
Tim Davis, drums

Steve Miller's parents were friends with Les Paul and Mary Ford, and when they visited, little Stevie Miller received some guitar lessons at a very young age from a master. Miller became an immensely popular international star playing "hot rod blues." From a beginning in Dallas, where he grew up, he moved to Chicago and eventually Los Angeles, playing in various bands of his own making throughout the process. In San Francisco, he, like so many others, gained his reputation through the Fillmore and the Avalon Ballroom. By the late sixties, the Steve Miller Band rose to national fame and has kept building popularity and recognition since.

Tracy Nelson, Irma Routen and the Earthettes

Vulcan Gas Company
August 15, 1969
Irma Routen, vocals; Jimmy Day, steel guitar;
Sadie Cantrell, vocals; Myrtice Fields, vocals;
John "Toad" Andrews, guitar; Tracy Nelson, vocals;
George Rains, drums; Bob Arthur, bass

Tracy Nelson had a strong background in folk, blues, and country prior to her association with Mother Earth. In the mid-sixties, she had recorded an album of traditional blues and spirituals. During the San Francisco years, she moved into more contemporary work to fit the times. After the Fillmore heyday, Mother Earth began to work a bit more country into their performances and albums. Although Mother Earth is now disbanded, Nelson is still a popular artist.

James Cotton

Vulcan Gas Company
October 8, 1969
Luther Tucker, guitar;
James Cotton, vocals and harmonica;
Sam Lay, drums; Robert Anderson, bass

From an early start at age nine, Cotton built a sizeable reputation for himself. He began with Sonny Boy Williamson and spent several years with Muddy Waters.

Mance Lipscomb
Vulcan Gas Company
October 8, 1969

Mance Lipscomb and James Cotton

James Cotton

Palmer Auditorium, Austin, Texas
November 5, 1969

In late 1969, a huge crowd packed Austin's Municipal Auditorium to cheer Johnny Winter in a triumphant return concert with James Cotton.

Johnny Winter

Palmer Auditorium, Austin, Texas
November 5, 1969

After exposure in *Rolling Stone*, the Johnny Winter Trio received requests to play all over the country as well as abroad, including an appearance at the famous Woodstock Festival.

Edgar Winter

Palmer Auditorium
November 5, 1969

While Johnny was playing, the audience wondered about a number of instruments lying unplayed about the stage. After an hour, Johnny introduced his then-unknown brother Edgar, who proceeded to move from saxophone to piano to drums to guitar with astounding proficiency and energy. No one there doubted that the Winters had another star. Edgar quickly gained fame along with his brother, then on his own with his bands White Trash and the Edgar Winter Group, with whom Boz Scaggs played for a brief while.

Hub City Movers

Vulcan Gas Company
December 26, 1969
Jimmie Dale Gilmore, guitar/vocals; Stuart Irvin, guitar;
Jerry Barnett, drums; Pat Pankratz, guitar;
Ed Vizard, saxophone; Charlie Sauer, bass

The Hub City Movers played an interesting game of musical chairs. Their first incarnation, known as the T. Nickel House Band, was based in Lubbock in 1966. Members included Jimmie Dale Gilmore, Jesse Hercules Taylor (later with Kracker Jack), John Reed (Freda and the Firedogs), Tiny McFarland (Alvin Crow), and Joe Ely. The band moved to San Francisco and, like so many other Texas bands making that move, dissolved upon contact. The Hub City Movers again surfaced in Austin. Band members were Gilmore, McFarland, Reed, Ed Vizard, and Ike Ritter. After their disbandment, Gilmore formed a new group, called the Flatlanders, which included such talent as Joe Ely and Butch Hancock.

44 中

Shiva's Headband

Vulcan Gas Company
February 11, 1970
Shawn Siegel
Spencer Perskin
Kenny Parker
Jerry Barnett
Susan Perskin

Johnny Winter

Vulcan Gas Company
March 10, 1970

Blind Smith

Vulcan Gas Company
March 28, 1970

Another relative unknown, Blind Smith was a singer and performer for most of his life. Smith played the Vulcan on several occasions with his all-white band—all in their teens—under the name Blind Guitar Smitty and the Tornadoes.

Hub City Movers

Vulcan Gas Company
March 28, 1970
Jimmie Dale Gilmore, guitar; Charlie Sauer, bass;
Jerry Barnett, drums; Ed Vizard, saxophone; Ike Ritter, guitar

New Riders of the Purple Sage

The Matrix, San Francisco, California
August 1970
Mickey Hart, drums; Dave Torbert, bass;
John Marmaduke Dawson, guitar/vocals;
David Nelson, guitar; Jerry Garcia, pedal steel

The New Riders of the Purple Sage were a Grateful Dead offshoot formed in the late sixties consisting of John Marmaduke Dawson, David Nelson, Jerry Garcia, Mickey Hart, and Dave Torbert. They later had a gold record with *The Adventures of Panama Red.*

Janis Joplin

The Matrix in San Francisco
August 18, 1970

Volumes have been written about the tortured songs and life of Janis Joplin, but little has been mentioned of her concern for the careers of her friends. This photo was taken backstage at an "All-Texas" night at the Matrix in San Francisco. She had slipped in unnoticed and sat obscured in darkness to watch her friend Julie Paul (who had originally introduced her to Threadgill) sing with Cross Country, who shared the bill with Boz Scaggs and Kracker Jack. At the Threadgill picnic, Janis had flatly predicted a great career for a then completely unknown composer/singer named Kris Kristofferson, who wrote her hit "Me and Bobby McGee." She died six weeks after this photo was taken.

Armadillo World Headquarters
September 10, 1970

Julie Paul and Cross Country

New Orleans Club
September 21, 1970

Freddie King
Backstage at Armadillo World Headquarters
October 3, 1970

*Crowd scene at
Freddie King concert*

*Corner 19th and San Antonio streets
Austin, Texas
October 3, 1970*

In 1971 Shiva's Headband was playing every now and then at the Armadillo, and Jim Franklin did a painting on a regular-sized canvas to use for a poster and handbills. At the same time, Capitol Records put out a Shiva's Headband album. They thought the painting would make a good advertising piece, and so they bought it from Franklin, blew it up to billboard size, and put it up for display in the main hall at Armadillo World Headquarters. They had bought five billboard spaces around town and decided to use it for one of them. It just happened to share space with Governor Preston Smith, who was running for re-election.

*Armadillo World Headquarters
October 2, 1970
Jamie Bassett, bass
Denny Freeman, guitar
Otis Lewis, drums
Freddie King*

ZZ Top

Armadillo World Headquarters
November 7, 1970
Dusty Hill, bass; Frank Beard, drums; Billy Gibbons, guitar

The most persistent—and eventually the most famous—of the Texas psychedelic rock bands, ZZ Top went from local interest in the early seventies to the ranks of the superstars within a few years. Billy Gibbons played earlier in The Moving Sidewalks. Dusty Hill and Frank Beard appeared in a group called American Blues, who brought attention to themselves by dying their hair blue.

Lightnin' Hopkins

Armadillo World Headquarters
November 13, 1970
Rex Bell, bass; Lightnin' Hopkins, vocals, guitar; Uncle John Turner, drums

Bluesman Sam "Lightnin'" Hopkins was born March 15, 1912, in Centerville, Texas. His career stretched from the 1920s up to the 1980s.

He had the ability to improvise music to fit whatever situation he found himself in. His hits include "Tee Model Blues," "Coffee Blues," and the rocking "Lightnin's Boogie." He died January 30, 1982, in Houston.

Because of his flexibility, Lightnin' Hopkins was an accessible and durable performer throughout his career. He began in the thirties alongside Blind Lemon Jefferson and Texas Alexander. Although the adjusting of his style to fit the times has tainted his "purity" in the minds of some blues fans, he had a tremendous impact on younger artists from Dylan to the Beatles.

Kracker Jack

Armadillo World Headquarters
December 16, 1970
Jesse Taylor, guitar; Tommy Shannon, bass;
Uncle John Turner, drums; Bruce Bowen, vocals;
Mike Kindred, keyboards

During the early to mid-seventies, Kracker Jack was an extremely popular rock band in Austin. They played many concerts with nationally famous bands and packed clubs around the area regularly. Two members of the group, Tommy Shannon and Uncle John Turner, originally played with the young Johnny Winter.

Shiva's Headband

Armadillo World Headquarters
December 27, 1970
Shawn Siegel, Spencer Perskin, Leo Bud, Ike Ritter, Mike Cooper

Jim Franklin
Resident artist at
Armadillo World
Headquarters
May 13, 1971

Storm

Armadillo World Headquarters
February 28, 1971
Lewis Cowdrey, harmonica; Jimmie Vaughan, guitar;
Doyle Bramhall, vocals; Otis Lewis, drums; Danny Galindo, bass

Doug Kershaw

Armadillo World Headquarters
January 2, 1971

Kershaw has played the fiddle and written songs since the age of five on the Louisiana bayous. In the early sixties, he recorded "Louisiana Man" with his brother as Rusty and Doug. The record reached the popular charts, but they sank back into obscurity quickly. A few years later, he was discovered by Johnny Cash and rose to immediate fame with his frantic style and stage antics.

Doug Kershaw
Mural at Armadillo World Headquarters
By Jim Franklin

Fats Domino

Armadillo World Headquarters
February 28, 1971
Herb Hardesty, saxophone

Among the most interesting Armadillo concerts were the two nights that Fats Domino and his band performed. He had been pounding the ivories and singing his original style of pop-blues for years and years—so long, in fact, that middle-aged folk, who had danced to his hit "Blueberry Hill" when they were in high school, brought their teenaged children to hear the music that had been popular when they were young.

While onstage, Fats wore a deep purple suit, satin shoes, and on his right ring finger, a diamond ring that could choke a horse.

Fats was very friendly and welcomed me backstage, where a six-foot-four-inch valet/bodyguard attended to him every minute. There were five or six people in the room, and Fats chatted constantly with them as the valet slipped the ring from his finger and put it away, slipped off his velvet jacket and carefully hung it up, removed his tie and silk shirt, unbuckled his belt, pulled his pants down, sat him in a chair, and removed his shoes and trousers.

Fats, in his socks and underwear, continued talking just as though nothing had happened. Two women were allowed into the room, and each asked him to autograph one of her breasts, which he was happy to do, but it never altered his conversation with the people asking him questions and writing in little notebooks.

Travis Holland and Michael Murphey

Armadillo World Headquarters
March 7, 1971

Coming out of several years of studio writing in Los Angeles, Michael Murphey moved back to Texas and began to record and perform his own work. He quickly gained attention and became known as the "Cosmic Cowboy," from his own satiric song by that name.

Jerry Jeff Walker

Armadillo World Headquarters
March 7, 1971

Best known for his composition "Mr. Bojangles," Walker has been interested in folk and country blues since childhood. After several years of trying out one niche or another, he finally found fame in the progressive-country brand of music from Central Texas. He adopted Austin, as have many such artists, performing locally and touring nationally.

Robert Shaw and Mance Lipscomb
Armadillo World Headquarters
March 20, 1971

Robert Shaw

Armadillo World Headquarters
March 20, 1971

Perhaps not as well-known to the general public as some of the other bluesmen, Shaw is highly regarded as "the King of the Barrelhouse Piano." He has appeared internationally at jazz and blues festivals and was frequently "rediscovered" in his native Austin by younger audiences.

He was one of the great Texas piano players. In his younger days, he started in Houston's Fifth Ward and worked what was called the Santa Fe circuit, singing the blues and playing barrelhouse, belly rubs, and stomps in small joints. With the coming of jukeboxes, there was less demand for his playing, so he settled down in Austin and opened Shaw's Food Market. He sold groceries and the best barbecue you ever ate. It was President Lyndon Johnson's favorite place, and he said, "Shaw's spare ribs and hot gut were the best anywhere."

I heard Robert play many times, and it was always a thrill. One time at the Armadillo, he did a whole set of ragtime. During the break, I told him I had never heard him play ragtime before, and he said he didn't play it very often because it is too much work to play rag.

The Fabulous Furry Freak Brothers

A Wall Mural at Armadillo World Headquarters
Painted by Gilbert Shelton
March 20, 1971
Phineas, Fat Freddie, Freewheelin' Franklin,
and Fat Freddie's Cat

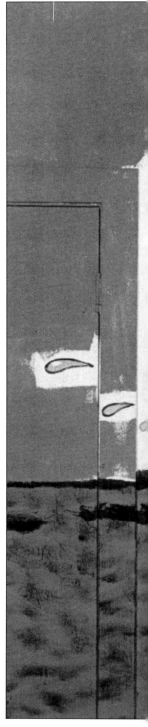

Gilbert Shelton explains, "The Fabulous Furry Freak Brothers were not actually based on specific real people. Before I did the first Freak Brothers page, I had done a five-minute, black-and-white, sixteen-millimeter film with my friend Renee Tooley, who was a film student at UT at the time, called *The Texas Hippies March on the Capitol,* starring Joe E. Brown. I used the first Freak Brothers page—the one about the giant magic marijuana seed—as a flyer for the film, which I was going to show at the Vulcan Gas Company. Everyone liked the comic strip better than the film. Bill Bramer later lost the only copy of the film, loaning it to somebody. I had originally called the character Freewheelin' Frank, but when I found out there was a San Francisco Hell's Angel by that name, I changed it quickly to Franklin. Fat Freddy? Charlie Pritchard had the nickname, but Ed Guinn had the avoirdupois. As for Phineas, like all fictional characters, they are a mixture of the writer and his friends. At least one story, the one where Phineas says he can't give all his money to the robbers, is a supposedly true story told to me about himself by Bud Shrake."

Three Faces West

Chequered Flag
April 15, 1971
Rick Fowler, Wayne Kidd, Ray Wylie Hubbard

A popular folk-rock group around Austin during the early seventies, Three Faces West began moving into the country-rock area earlier than many others. They are mainly notable for the introduction of Ray Wylie Hubbard to the local scene. Later he gained wide recognition for his satiric composition "Up Against the Wall, Redneck Mother," which became a theme song of sorts for progressive country. Hubbard can never escape a performance without a rendition of this number.

Angela Strehli with James Polk and the Brothers

Ascot Room, Austin
May 12, 1971
John Reed, guitar; Don Lupo, bass; JoAnn, back-up vocals;
James Polk, saxophone; Angela Strehli; Hambone;
Phil Richardson, trombone; Martin Banks, trumpet;
Matthew Robinson, guitar

Flying Burrito Brothers

Armadillo World Headquarters
June 4, 1971
Rick Roberts, Bernie Leadon, Chris Hillman,
Michael Clarke, Al Perkins

Leo Kottke
Armadillo World Headquarters
August 4, 1971

Ravi Shankar
Armadillo World Headquarters
October 9, 1971
Alla Rakha, tabla
Ravi Shankar, sitar
Kamala, tambura

Mance Lipscomb, Bill Neely, and Taj Mahal

Backstage, Armadillo World Headquarters
October 22, 1971

Although young and from an urban middle-class background, Taj Mahal has been influential in reviving the older, rustic blues. He studied the styles of artists such as Mance Lipscomb and then perfected them himself. He gained his major fame through recordings of simple, traditional acoustic-guitar blues, but branched out into electric guitar backed by a full band.

John Sebastian and wife Catherine

Armadillo World Headquarters
October 29, 1971

John Sebastian gained fame as a founding member of The
Lovin' Spoonful. Their hits included "Summer in the City,"
"Darlin' Be Home Soon," "Nashville Cats," "Do You Believe in
Magic?" and "Daydream."

His most memorable solo performance was captured on
film in the movie *Woodstock*.

The Spoonful were elected to the Rock and Roll Hall of
Fame, Class of 2000.

Vassar Clements and Earl Scruggs

With Gary Scruggs
November 5, 1971

Backstage at Armadillo World Headquarters
November 5, 1971

Vassar Clements, a superb bluesy bluegrass fiddler, was instrumental in broadening the scope and popularity of the older idioms by combining them with newer styles. He performed with the Earl Scruggs Review and with Jerry Garcia's bluegrass band, Old and In the Way.

Earl Scruggs reached wide fame, first with Bill Monroe's band, then with longtime partner Lester Flatt. When they split up, Scruggs put together the Earl Scruggs Review with his sons and a number of other young performers, playing a more contemporary rock-country sound.

Cheech and Chong
Armadillo World Headquarters
March 12, 1972
Tommy Chong, Cheech Marin

Greezy Wheels

Armadillo World Headquarters
March 8, 1972
Cleve Hattersley, guitar; Mary Egan, violin; Tony Laier, drums;
Mike Pugh, bass; Lissa Hattersley, vocals; Pat Pankratz, guitar

The most popular band in Austin during the first half of the seventies, Greezy Wheels embodied the perfect synthesis of psychedelic consciousness and traditional country sensibilities. It was hard to find any major Austin concert where Greezy Wheels was not on the bill and wildly applauded.

Bill Graham
Armadillo World Headquarters
February 5, 1972

Bill Graham, lecturing at the Armadillo, was the most prolific promoter of music in the 1960s, 1970s, and 1980s.

Eddie Wilson
Impresario of
Armadillo World
Headquarters
April 13, 1972

Kenneth Threadgill

Bevo's, Austin
April 27, 1972

Kenneth Threadgill was a legend in his own time singing those old Jimmie Rodgers railroad songs.

In the early 1930s, he ran a service station on North Lamar Boulevard. In December 1933, when Prohibition was repealed, he got the first license in Travis County to sell beer. It was just a filling station, but he started selling snacks like crackers and rat cheese to workmen who came by, and longnecks were two for a quarter.

In the early 1960s, it got to be a popular place for young people to hang out, drink beer, play guitars, and sing those old blues songs with Kenneth Threadgill.

Janis Joplin was at the University of Texas then. Threadgill's offered her one of her first chances to sing in public. She and Kenneth became very good friends. Some years later, a lot of his friends had a big picnic honoring him, and Janis flew in from Hawaii to attend it.

Shawn Phillips
Armadillo World Headquarters
May 12, 1972

Guy Clark
Castle Creek
June 13, 1972

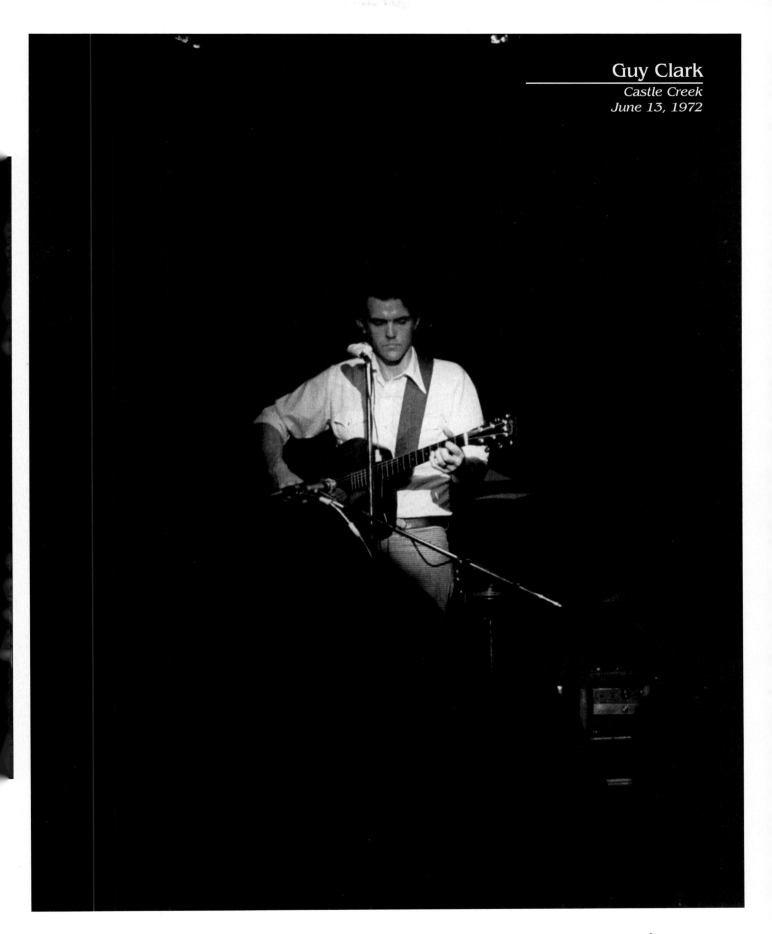

Fanny

Armadillo World Headquarters
July 14, 1972
Nickey Barclay, keyboard; Jean Millington, bass;
Alice De Buhr, drums; June Millington, guitar

The first all-girl rock band, Fanny appeared on Barbra Streisand's
album *Stoney End*.

Angela and Hard Times

Rolling Hills, Austin, Texas
August 4, 1972
W. C. Clark, guitar; Angela Strehli; Denny Freeman, guitar;
Andy Miller, drums; Alex Napier, bass

Freda and the Firedogs

Beer Garden, Armadillo World Headquarters
July 30, 1972
David Cook, Steve McDaniels, Marcia Ball,
Bobby Earl Smith, John Reed

August 6, 1972
Lewis Cowdrey,
Paul Ray,
Ed Vizard,
Jimmie Vaughan,
Doyle Bramhall,
Jeff Barnes

Storm

At Hungry Horse
August 5, 1972
Paul Ray, Doyle Bramhall, Jeff Barnes, Ed Vizard, Jimmie Vaughan, Lewis Cowdrey

Another popular band of the mid-seventies, Storm included a number of well-known Austin musicians. Lewis Cowdrey fronted the popular Austin dance band Lewis and the Legends. Paul Ray went on to form The Cobras, which featured Stevie Ray Vaughan on guitar. Ed Vizard recorded and performed with western-swing band Asleep at the Wheel and was a mainstay in the Austin live-music scene. Doyle Bramhall became a songwriter and co-wrote several songs for Stevie Ray and Double Trouble. Jimmie Vaughan founded the Fabulous Thunderbirds and has a successful solo career. Jeff Barnes became a member of the Grammy award–winning nuclear polka band Brave Combo.

Lewis Cowdrey, Sally Adams, Diana Ray,
Paul Ray, Ed Vizard, Doyle Bramhall,
Jimmie Vaughan, Jeff Barnes

Dan Hicks and His Hot Licks

Armadillo World Headquarters
August 9, 1972
Sid Page, violin; John Girton, guitar; Jaime Leopold, bass;
Maryann Price, vocals; Dan Hicks, guitar/vocals;
Naomi Ruth Eisenberg, violins/vocals

In the early Haight-Ashbury scene, a band called the Charlatans was assembled and grew to rapid stardom playing blues, jug-band tunes, and some rock with an easygoing style. The drummer was Dan Hicks. As the San Francisco scene became heavier, Hicks' taste followed suit, and after a while the group broke up. After that, Hicks assembled his own band, the Hot Licks, and put together a flashy, satirical stage show harking back to older swing styles of the forties.

Willie Nelson

Armadillo World Headquarters
August 12, 1972

Willis Alan Ramsey
Armadillo World Headquarters
September 3, 1972

Although an excellent musician and lyricist, Ramsey has never reached big stardom, which is the way he wants it. However, with a deep-seated interest in traditional white southern blues, he has attracted a lot of attention with his sensitive songs and easy delivery. Many of his songs have been recorded by others, including his most famous composition, "Muskrat Candlelight," recorded by Captain and Tennille as "Muskrat Love."

B. W. Stevenson
Castle Creek
September 13, 1972

Singer/songwriter famous for writing the songs "Shambala," recorded by Three Dog Night, and "My Maria," a hit for Brooks and Dunn.

Seals and Crofts

Armadillo World Headquarters
September 3, 1972
Dash Crofts, Jim Seals

This popular duet's hits include "Diamond Girl," "We May Never Pass This Way Again," and "Summer Breeze." Both were originally in the group The Champs, famous for their hit "Tequila."

中 97

Freda and the Firedogs

The Friend Factory
September 16, 1972
Bobby Earl Smith, John Reed, Steve McDaniels,
David Cook, Marcia Ball

The Flatlanders

October 6, 1972
Rev. Steve Wesson, autoharp; Tony Pearson, mandolin;
Butch Hancock, guitar/vocals; Joe Ely, guitar;
John Reed, bass

Peter Frampton
Armadillo World Headquarters
October 6, 1972
(at left)

Steve Miller
Palmer Auditorium
October 9, 1972

Lowell Fulson

Armadillo World Headquarters
October 9, 1972

Fulson served an apprenticeship with Texas Alexander in the late thirties and came into his own by the late forties and early fifties. Like many others, he adapted his style to rock in the later years. When he reached the height of his popularity in the early fifties, his piano player was a young blind man named Ray Charles.

Jerry Lee Lewis
Armadillo World Headquarters
October 14, 1972
Bill Campbell, guitar

Goose Creek Symphony

Armadillo World Headquarters
October 28, 1972
Willard, Cactus Jimmy, Charlie Gearheart,
Flash, Flyin' Fred, Paul Spradlin

Goose Creek Symphony's Kentucky background plays an important role in the sound they made popular in the mid-seventies. Although most of their songs are original compositions by band member Charlie Gearheart, they are in the style of traditional mountain music of the South.

Steely Dan

Armadillo World Headquarters
October 28, 1972
Jeff "Skunk" Baxter, guitar; Walter Becker, bass;
Jim Hodder, drums; David Palmer, vocals;
Denny Dias, guitar; Donald Fagen, keyboards

New Riders of the Purple Sage

Armadillo World Headquarters
September 2, 1974
David Torbert, bass; John Marmaduke
Dawson, guitar; David Nelson, guitar;
Spencer Dryden, drums

Boz Scaggs

Armadillo World Headquarters
November 3, 1972
Charles Chalmers, tenor sax

Enthralled with the blues at an early age, Scaggs played around Dallas for years with limited success. In the late sixties, he joined Steve Miller's band, where he began drawing attention and developing his own work. After a short stint with Edgar Winter, he broke away on his own in the early seventies.

Willie Nelson

Armadillo World Headquarters
November 4, 1972

In the late fifties and early sixties, Nelson was a successful songwriter in Nashville, penning such hits as "Crazy" and "Hello Walls." His crossover into performing was moderately successful, but big fame eluded him until he landed in Austin in the early seventies. This was a time when various local groups were experimenting with traditional country combined with blues and rock, and Nelson served as a catalyst, becoming the spiritual leader of this new sound of progressive country.

Grateful Dead

Palmer Auditorium
November 22, 1972
Keith Godchaux, keyboards
Bob Weir, guitar/vocals
Jerry Garcia, lead gutiar
Bill Kreutzman, drums
Phil Lesh, bass

Grateful Dead

Palmer Auditorium
November 22, 1972
Phil Lesh, bass—standing; Keith Godchaux; Jerry Garcia, guitar;
Bob Weir, guitar; Bill Kreutzman, drums

On Thanksgiving Day, in the early afternoon, Eddie Wilson phoned me from the Armadillo World Headquarters. He said that the Dead and others had come in and to grab my Nikon and come on down.

I was there in a few minutes and went to the upstairs room, a big room that was away from everything and used for storage and whatever. There were about twenty people standing around talking and smoking.

Eddie introduced me to Jerry Garcia, and we met like old friends. Of course, I knew all about him, and he knew about me from my son Minor, who had a guitar shop in San Francisco then. Jerry and the rest of the Dead hung out occasionally at Minor's shop while he worked on any number of instruments that needed repair.

Jerry introduced me to Phil Lesh, who played bass guitar for the Dead, and said, "This is Minor's father."

As we shook hands, Phil said, "When is my guitar going to be ready?"

That question sort of stopped me, and I said, "I don't know, I'll ask him the next time I talk with him."

A lot of the people gathered there were musicians, and they decided to jam for a while, so everyone drifted down to the stage. That afternoon, one of the most incredible super-groups ever assembled in the Armadillo performed their one and only show together.

This was the band: Jerry Garcia on the pedal steel guitar; Leon Russell on piano and vocals; Phil Lesh on bass; Sweet Mary Egan of Greezy Wheels on violin; Benny Thurman (once a member of the legendary 13th Floor Elevators) on fiddle; Jerry Barnett, from Shiva's Headband, on drums; and Doug Sahm on guitar and vocals. The doors were open to all, and people just wandered in on this unannounced show to enjoy a truly great, free, almost-three-hour performance.

Armadillo World Headquarters
November 23, 1972
After-concert gathering at Armadillo World Headquarters
Members of the Grateful Dead, Doug Sahm, Eddie Wilson, and others.

A Free Thanksgiving Day Jam Session
Armadillo World Headquarters
November 23, 1972
Leon Russell, Benny Thurman, Mary Egan, Phil Lesh,
Jerry Barnett, Jerry Garcia, Doug Sahm

With Billy Joe Shaver

With Ralph Mooney—steel guitar

Waylon Jennings

Armadillo World Headquarters
December 1, 1972

From an early start as one of Buddy Holly's backup musicians immediately before Holly's death, Jennings became a Nashville regular in the country field. However, like Willie Nelson, he didn't really fit, and he moved into more progressive country, forming with Nelson the nucleus of the Austin sound, a combination of traditional country with more recent rock beats.

Storm

Armadillo World Headquarters
December 13, 1972
Jimmie Vaughan, guitar; Mike Kindred, keyboards;
Paul Ray, bass; Freddie Walden, drums

Bill Neely

4th and Trinity streets, Austin, Texas
January 20, 1973

In a period of rediscovery of white country roots, Neely, like Threadgill, is of the generation that learned the railroad blues of Jimmie Rodgers and others firsthand. Well-known in Central Texas, he became a fixture in the Austin area, playing most of the clubs and performing with many of the national blues names.

Gram Parsons

Armadillo World Headquarters
February 21, 1973

With a strong background in country
blues, having grown up in the South,
Parsons was instrumental in turning
the Byrds toward a more country direc-
tion when he joined them in the late
sixties. The move may have been a bit
premature, but when he left to form the
Flying Burrito Brothers, the popularity
of country-rock was in full bloom, and
the Burrito Brothers enjoyed a huge
reputation until Parsons faded from the
group for health reasons. Before his
untimely death in 1973, he sang with
Emmylou Harris.

Gram Parsons and Emmylou Harris

Armadillo World Headquarters
February 21, 1973
Neil Flanz, steel guitar

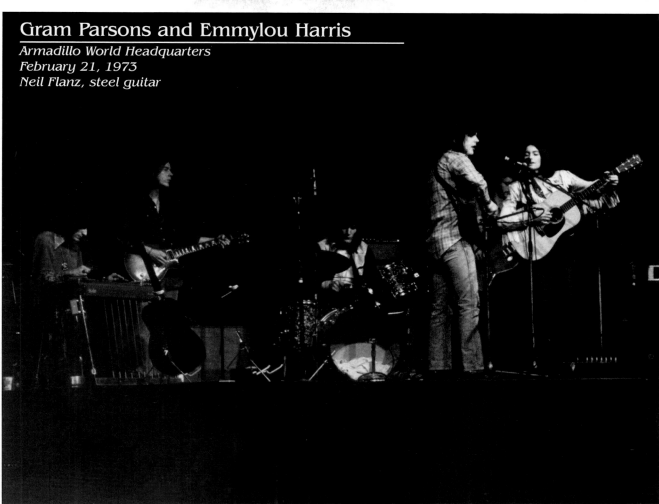

Backstage with
Jim Franklin's
Armadillo helmet

Kinky Friedman and the Texas Jewboys

Armadillo World Headquarters
March 22, 1973

With a unique blend of blues, rock, country, and sardonic satire, Friedman carved out a unique niche for himself. His first group went by the title of King Arthur and the Carrots. As the "Texas Jewboy," he used heavy-handed but infectious humor to make his statements, at the same time employing good music and musicians to keep from being just a novelty act.

Years later, he became a successful mystery writer.

Bette Midler with Barry Manilow on Piano

Armadillo World Headquarters
March 24, 1973

Willie Nelson

*Armadillo World
Headquarters
April 7, 1973
Jimmy Day, pedal steel;
Paul English, drums;
Bee Spears, bass;
Willie Nelson*

中 125

John McLaughlin and the Mahavishnu Orchestra

Armadillo World Headquarters
April 5, 1973
Billy Cobham, drums; John McLaughlin, Gibson double-neck guitar (12 over 6);
Rick Laird, bass; Jan Hammer, keyboards

J. Geils Band

Armadillo World Headquarters
April 19, 1973
Magic Dick, harmonica; J. Geils, guitar; Peter Wolf, vocals;
Stephen Bladd, drums; Dan Klein, bass; Seth Justman, keys

Based in Boston, the J. Geils Band made a huge impression on the national
scene during the mid-seventies with several hit albums and successful tours.
Muddy Waters called their harmonica player, Magic Dick, the best white man
in the business. Along with lead singer Peter Wolf, they created the heavy
metal fusion of blues and rock that made them so popular.

Balcones Fault

Armadillo World Headquarters
April 21, 1973
Steve Blodgett, bass; Michael McGeary, drums;
Jack Jacobs, guitar/vocals; Fletcher Clark, guitar/vocals

This band was extremely popular in Austin during the first half of the seventies. In a period when music was going in many different directions and bands were becoming more polarized, Balcones Fault was successful due to the eclectic nature of its repertoire. They played everything from Broadway hits to country to reggae.

Doug Sahm

Soap Creek
May 6, 1973
Jack Barber, bass; Augie Meyers, guitar;
Doug Sahm; Rocky Morales, sax;
David Cook, steel

From an early start as Little Doug Sahm, through national fame as the Sir Douglas Quintet, to later fame with the Texas Tornadoes, Sahm became a genuine Texas legend. He roamed the musical spectrum from mod rock to Tex-Mex blues.

He died suddenly of a heart attack in Taos, New Mexico, on November 18, 1999.

Joy of Cooking

Armadillo World Headquarters
May 12, 1973
David Garthwaite, bass. backup vocals
Terry Garthwaite, guitar/vocals
Fritz Kasten, drums/sax
Toni Brown, keyboards

Willie Nelson

Country Music Revival, Victoria, Texas
June 17, 1973
Mickey Raphael, harmonica
Willie Nelson, guitar/vocals

Texoid
Country Music Revival, Victoria, Texas
June 17, 1973
Ed Guinn, keyboard
Bob Brown, guitar and vocals
Michael McGeary, drums
Stan Coppinger, bass
unknown, steel guitar

Mose Allison
Armadillo World Headquarters
June 22, 1973

Willie Nelson's First Fourth of July Picnic
1973
Dripping Springs, Texas

Willie Nelson's Picnic

Dripping Springs
July 4, 1973

John Prine

Waylon Jennings

Sammi Smith

Asleep At The Wheel

Armadillo World Headquarters
September 7, 1973
Lucky Oceans, pedal steel
Ray Benson, guitar/vocals
Leroy Preston, drums; Gene Dobkin, bass
Chris O'Connell, guitar/vocals
Floyd Domino, piano (not pictured)

Reaching back to Bob Wills' Texas swing, Asleep at the Wheel gained a big following across the country as well as wild enthusiasm in its adopted home of Austin. Working in traditional modes, they added a number of original songs to continue to expand the style's appeal to younger audiences.

Tom T. Hall

Armadillo World Headquarters
November 14, 1973

Although generally categorized as a pure country performer, Hall gained a broad following with his ballads, some of them blues-ish, others in a light-hearted vein. His easygoing style lent itself well to acceptance by the progressive-country audiences of Austin.

Willie Nelson and Tom T. Hall
Mickey Raphael on harp

Van Morrison

Armadillo World Headquarters
January 10, 1974

Strangely enough, growing up in his native
Ireland, Morrison cultivated a strong interest in
American blues and country music. He learned
to play saxophone and guitar early and played
in a number of bands while still in school. In his
English rock days, he gained wide fame with his
band, Them, and their hit "Gloria." By the end
of the sixties, he disbanded the group and went
on to great popularity as an individual artist,
getting more into blues-rock.

Tracy Nelson and Mother Earth

Armadillo World Headquarters
January 13, 1974
Bob Arthur, bass; John "Toad" Andrews, guitar;
Tracy Nelson, vocals

Asleep At The Wheel

Armadillo World Headquarters
February 1, 1974
Floyd Domino, Tony Garnier, Chris O'Connell,
Leroy Preston, Richard Casanova,
Ray Benson, Lucky Oceans

Commander Cody and His Lost Planet Airmen

Armadillo World Headquarters
February 1, 1974
George "Commander Cody" Frayne, keys; Buffalo Bruce Barlow, bass;
Bill Kirchen, guitar; Lance Dickerson, drums; Billy C. Farlow, guitar/vocals;
Andy Stein, fiddle; John Tichy, guitar; unknown, pedal steel

A California band by way of Ann Arbor, Commander Cody and His Lost Planet Airmen gained wide fame as a country-rock-parody band. The band performed regularly at the Armadillo and cut a live album there.

Linda Ronstadt

Backstage at Armadillo World Headquarters
February 6, 1974
Bruce Barlow, bass
Linda Ronstadt
Andy Stein, fiddle
Herb Steiner
Billy Kirchen
John Tichy

Little Feat

Armadillo World Headquarters
February 8, 1974
Billy Payne, Paul Barrere, Richie Hayward, Lowell George,
Kenny Gradney, Sam Clayton

A West Coast band for years, Little Feat rose to national prominence with a number of albums of a variety of sounds. Lowell George, famous for his song "Willin'," came from the Mothers of Invention, and drummer Richie Hayward was formerly with the folk-rock band Fraternity of Man.

Texoid
Armadillo World Headquarters
February 8, 1974
Ed Guinn, Stan Coppinger, Bob Brown

Greezy Wheels
Armadillo World
Headquarters
March 15, 1974
Pat Pankratz,
Cleve Hattersley,
Mike Pugh, Mary Egan,
Tony Laier, Tony Airoldi,
Lissa Hattersley

Bruce Springsteen

Armadillo World Headquarters
March 15, 1974

On March 15, 1974, at a concert in the AWHQ, I was standing backstage chatting with Bruce Springsteen before he went on. All of a sudden, three very attractive young women burst into the room, and with them was one of the guards from the backstage door. That door was always guarded during a concert, and it was virtually impossible to get through it without a pass. This trio had pleaded with the guards that they had a gift for Springsteen and insisted on giving it to him themselves. The guards were sympathetic and said they could go in but stay only a couple of minutes, and to make sure, one would go with them.

It was Rosie herself and two other beauties. They moved like the wind, slipped off his jacket, put this T-shirt on him, giggled, and left. He stood there, stunned. I said, "Bruce, we have got to document this." He agreed, so I posed him against a blank wall and took this photograph.

About six weeks after this, he gained national recognition when he appeared on the cover of both *Time* and *Newsweek* magazines simultaneously!

Danny Federici, keyboards
Clarence "The Big Man" Clemons, sax
Bruce Springsteen, guitar
Garry Tallent, bass

Genesis

Armadillo World Headquarters
First American Tour
March 17, 1974
Tony Banks, guitar; Mike Rutherford, guitar/bass;
Peter Gabriel, vocals; Phil Collins, drums; Steve Hackett, piano

Michael Martin Murphey
Armadillo World Headquarters
March 23, 1974

Brewer and Shipley
Armadillo World Headquarters
April 3, 1974
Tom Shipley, Mike Brewer

They were famous for their hit "One Toke Over the Line."

Dr. John

Armadillo World Headquarters
April 15, 1974

Growing up in New Orleans during the forties and fifties, Dr.
John had deep roots in black blues. At fifteen he began
working as a studio musician and ended up backing almost
every one of the legendary performers recording in New
Orleans. Later on he began incorporating more of the blues
into his act to become one of the best-known and most
highly respected white blues performers in the country.

Buffy Sainte-Marie

Armadillo World Headquarters
April 19, 1974

Freddie King
Armadillo World Headquarters
May 15, 1974

Doug Sahm
Armadillo World Headquarters
August 4, 1974

Too Smooth
Armadillo World Headquarters
September 11, 1974

Clifton Chenier, "King of Zydeco"

At Soap Creek Saloon
October 11, 1974

Harry Hypolite, Little Buck Senegal,
Cleveland Chenier, John Hart, Clifton Chenier

Roy Buchanan

Armadillo World Headquarters
September 18, 1974

Although well-known throughout the East for many years, Buchanan didn't reach general popularity until the mid-seventies. He has been called the best blues and rock guitarist in the business by many, and at one time was considered as a replacement for Mick Taylor when he left the Rolling Stones.

The Pointer Sisters

Armadillo World Headquarters
November 10, 1974
Bonnie, Ruth, and Anita Pointer

Born in Oakland, the sisters were raised in a fundamentalist church where they began singing in the choir. In the early seventies, they decided to try it professionally and began as a backup group to Elvin Bishop, Taj Mahal, Boz Scaggs, and many others. In 1973 they went off on their own and established themselves quickly with their wild, infectious renditions of many rhythm and blues and swing numbers from older days as well as their own compositions.

Bill Monroe and the Bluegrass Boys

Armadillo World Headquarters
November 22, 1974

Literally the father of bluegrass (named for his band, the Blue-grass Boys), Monroe created its unique sound by taking various elements of western swing, white gospel, and black blues banjo and fusing them together. Early members of his band included Chubby Wise, Lester Flatt, and Earl Scruggs.

John Lee Hooker

Antone's on Sixth Street
October 1, 1976
(Above) Hubert Sumlin, guitar; John Lee Hooker, guitar; Big Walter
"Shakey" Horton, harmonica; Andy Miller, drums; Eddie Taylor, guitar;
Keith Ferguson, bass (not pictured); Denny Freeman, piano (not pictured)

Perhaps the most modern of the older blues artists, Hooker had tremendous impact on rhythm and blues and on rock bands. He began using an electrical amplification system very early in his career and injected heavier doses of more driving boogie into his music than many of the other bluesmen. Most of the newer rhythm and blues bands studied his style, and many performed with him.

Grey Ghost

Victory Grill
June 19, 1987

The first time I heard Grey Ghost was at the Victory Grill. He was one of the old-time, almost-forgotten musicians that Tary Owens rediscovered and encouraged to play and sing the blues again. Roosevelt Thomas "Grey Ghost" Williams was eighty-four years old when I took this photograph, and he had been performing since 1918.

Marcia Ball

La Zona Rosa
July 2, 1991
Paul Klemperer, sax; Steve Williams, guitar; Rodney Craig, drums; Marcia Ball,
piano/vocals; Don Bennett, bass

After holding the center of very popular Austin band Freda and the Firedogs in the early seventies, Ball drifted toward the older country songs, singing with the Bronco Brothers and then with her own band, the Misery Brothers. She now plays nationally with her own band.

Toni Price

La Zona Rosa
September 25, 1991
Derek O'Brien
Toni Price
George Rains
Sarah Brown

Lavada Durst

La Zona Rosa, Austin, Texas
October 5, 1992

Lavada Durst had been Dr. Hepcat back in the 1950s and 1960s with a radio program that "laid down the cool" grooves for his brothers and sisters, playing the blues and contemporary black music. It was the first such radio program in Austin.

Emmylou Harris
La Zona Rosa
October 12, 1992

中 177

Dr. John
La Zona Rosa
October 17, 1992

John Mayall and the Bluesbreakers
La Zona Rosa
September 11, 1993

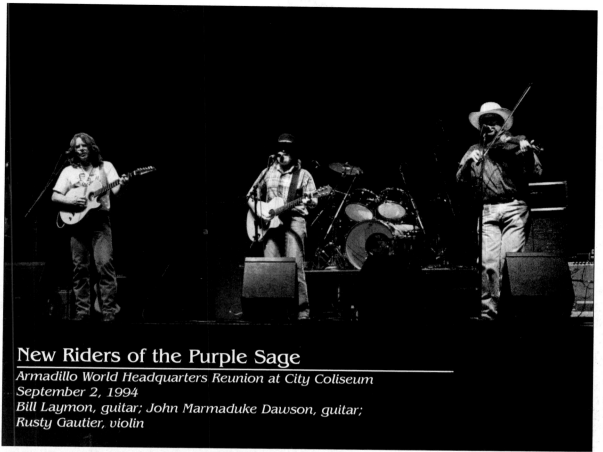

New Riders of the Purple Sage
Armadillo World Headquarters Reunion at City Coliseum
September 2, 1994
Bill Laymon, guitar; John Marmaduke Dawson, guitar;
Rusty Gautier, violin

Joe Ely
City Coliseum
September 2, 1994

Leon Russell

City Coliseum,
Austin, Texas
September 2, 1994
Teddy Jack Russell, guitar; unknown, bass;
Leon Russell, piano and vocals

The Flatlanders

City Coliseum
September 3, 1994
Jesse Taylor, Joe Ely,
Butch Hancock,
Jimmie Dale Gilmore

Lou Ann Barton with Derek O'Brien

City Coliseum
September 3, 1994

Augie Meyers

City Coliseum, Austin, Texas
September 3, 1994
Kevin Lewis, guitar
Clay Meyers, drums
Augie Meyers, vocals/accordion
Chris Holzhaus, guitar
Eric Hamilton, bass
Mike Saunders, trumpet
Sage Odem, piano
Ray Valencia, sax

Augie Meyers was the keyboard player with the Sir Douglas Quintet, founding member of the Texas Tornadoes, and the leader of his own band.

All-Star Jam
City Coliseum, Austin, Texas
September 3, 1994
Derek O'Brien, guitar; Tracy Nelson, vocals;
Glen Fukunaga, bass; Jake Andrews, guitar

中 183

Cover from one of Johnny Winter's early albums, released in 1969 by Imperial Records (story below).

JOHNNY WINTER

THE PROGRESSIVE BLUES EXPERIMENT

STEREO

LP-12431

IMPERIAL

After the Vulcan Gas Company had been open for a while, a record producer named Bill Josey started taping some shows there. He was middle-aged and very straight, and he had a small record company called Sonobeat Records. Josey had put out a few folk records that were popular at the time, but he was smart enough to realize that the new sounds coming from the Vulcan might be worth getting on tape. When the Johnny Winter Trio took the place by storm, he drew up a contract and started taping them.

Josey knew he would need pictures to go along with future record releases, so he asked around the Vulcan for who was the best photographer. They all said "Burton Wilson!", and so he called me.

Bill Josey knew exactly what he wanted for Johnny Winter. He wanted a background of seamless white paper and a standing pose of Johnny, dressed in his various hippie-style costumes, with a guitar, and nothing else. He was very definite about it.

I had everything set up when Johnny arrived with four or five outfits and as many guitars. I worked with 35mm and 2¼-by-2¼ cameras and took a lot of pictures. In the last pose, Johnny picked up an all-steel National guitar.

With only one exposure left in my camera, I just had to do my own thing. I asked him to hold it so that his face reflected on the back of the guitar, and I snapped the photo.

Bill Josey sold the whole package—recordings, photos, and all—to Imperial Records. When they put the album together, they used that picture for the front album cover and four of the other poses on the back cover.

They called it *Progessive Blues Experiment,* and it was Johnny Winter's first release. This is the kind of situation all photographers dream about.

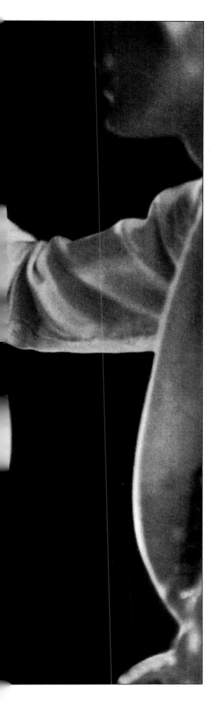

INDEX

*Vulcan Gas Company
poster by
Jim Franklin.*

(Above) Delmark Records release from 1961. (Below) Arhoolie Records' 1990 reissue of two of Big Joe Williams' 1960s albums on one CD.

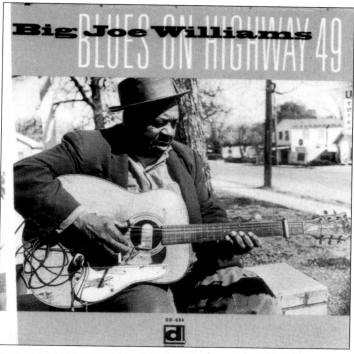

Collection of mid-sixties recordings featuring Mance Lipscomb, Blind Lemon Jefferson, and many of their peers, issued in 1993 by Catfish Records.

Multi-talented author/blues musician Keri Leigh's 1993 CD from Amazing Records.

Flip side of the 45 jacket I photographed for the Johnny Winter Trio, 1968.